Biography.

Mao
ZEDONG

Whitney Stewart

Twenty-First Century Books
Minneapolis

To my mother, who first took me to China

The author wishes to thank Sidney and Yulin Rittenberg for their hospitality and insights. Dorine Bosman, Paul Cassingham, Lolo Houbein, Maggie Huang, J. Alison James, Anika James, Michael Lestz, Geyshe Rinchen Choegyal, Justin Rudelson, Prescott Stewart, Cheryl Whitesel, and Lobsang Yeshi were all helpful. My editor, Mary Winget, always gives the right advice. My husband, Hans Andersson, and my son, Christoph, were patient and understanding as I worked.

Twenty-First Century Books
A division of Lerner Publishing Group
241 First Avenue North
Minneapolis, MN 55401 U.S.A.

Website address: www.lernerbooks.com

Library of Congress Cataloging-in-Publication Data

Stewart, Whitney, 1959–
    Mao Zedong / by Whitney Stewart.
        p.   cm. — (A&E biography)
    Includes bibliographical references and index.
    ISBN-13: 978–0–8225–2797–8 (lib. bdg. : alk. paper)
    ISBN-10: 0–8225–2797–9 (lib. bdg. : alk. paper)
    Mao Zedong, 1883–1976. 2. Heads of state—China—Biography. I. Title.
DS778M3.S7623   2006
951.05'092—dc22   2005008445

Manufactured in the United States of America
1 2 3 4 5 6 – BP – 11 10 09 08 07 06

CONTENTS

In Tiananmen Square, on October 1, 1949, Mao Zedong announced to a crowd of supporters that his Communist Party had gained control of China.

INTRODUCTION:
BUILDING A RED NATION

On October 1, 1949, Mao Zedong prepared to give a speech from the balcony of the Gate of Heavenly Peace, in Beijing's Tiananmen Square. This gate is the central entrance to the Forbidden City. For centuries China's emperors had lived and ruled there like gods, tucked away from ordinary citizens. Until the beginning of the twentieth century, few had dared to challenge the emperors. Those who had tried usually lost their heads.

But by the time Mao stood to greet the Chinese people, the country had changed dramatically. The people had lived through the fall of the last emperor, fighting among local military leaders (called warlords), war with Japan, and civil war. Mao and his peasant army had created a Communist nation. They promised the people a life free of starvation, unemployment, and unfair laws. They offered equal rights and education for all.

On this day, a crowd of one hundred thousand of Mao's supporters stood in Tiananmen Square waving banners, singing revolutionary songs, and shouting such slogans as "Long Live the Chinese Communist Party," and "Long Live the People's Republic of China."

While waiting for Mao, the crowd drew inspiration from a giant portrait of their leader. When they finally saw Mao stepping out onto the balcony, they shouted wildly. They believed in Mao. They believed he served the people, and they were full of hope. Li Zhisui, Mao's personal doctor, remembers seeing Mao for the first time:

> I was so full of joy my heart nearly burst out of my throat, and tears welled up in my eyes. I was proud of China, so full of hope.... I had no doubt that Mao was the great leader of the revolution.

Standing tall in his dark brown suit and simple worker's cap, Mao spoke into a large microphone. In his scratchy, high voice, he announced the founding of the People's Republic of China:

> The people throughout China have been plunged into bitter suffering and tribulations since the Chiang Kaishek Guomindang reactionary government betrayed the fatherland...and launched the counter-revolutionary war.... Now, the People's War of Liberation has been basically won, and the majority of the people in the country have been liberated (freed).

After his speech, Mao watched the parade below. The People's Liberation Army (PLA) marched by. Then came a line of army tanks. Behind the tanks marched a stream of civilians shouting "Long Live Chairman Mao," to which Mao answered, "Long Live the People's Republic."

As evening came and the sky darkened, fireworks exploded in the sky. Dancers carrying glowing lanterns whirled around the square as musicians played revolutionary songs. Mao's name echoed throughout China's capital city.

Mao was born in this thirteen-room mud-brick farmhouse in the village of Shaoshan, China, in 1893.

Chapter **ONE**

ANOINT THE EAST

MAO ZEDONG WAS BORN IN A MUD-BRICK HOUSE
with a thatched roof in 1893. It stood on a wooded
hillside near a lotus pond. December winds blew
through China's Shaoshan village as Mao's mother,
Wen Qimei, bundled her infant. Following Chinese
custom, she did not bathe her child for three days.
When he was four weeks old, she shaved his head
except for a small tuft of hair on the crown of his
head. This tuft held the baby firmly to life, or so tra-
dition said.

Mao's father, Mao Rensheng, an uneducated but
prospering rice farmer, called in a fortune-teller to
record the child's horoscope. After consulting the
man, Rensheng gave his son a name meaning "Anoint

the East." Rensheng looked upon Mao as the heir to the family name and growing rice business.

Rensheng lived with his wife, son, and father on two and a half acres of rice paddy. For a Chinese peasant living under imperial rule, he had a comfortable wealth.

Mao's affectionate mother had a gentle approach to raising children. She took Mao to the village temple and taught him the Buddhist principles of compassion and generosity. During times of famine, she often gave beggars rice, when her husband was not looking. He disapproved of charity.

In the family's large house, Mao had his own bedroom. So did his younger brother, Zemin, born two and a half years after Mao. Such privacy was rare in China, where most peasants lived crowded into one or two rooms.

By being thrifty, Mao's father saved enough money to buy another acre and to hire two workers to help on the farm. Once a month, Rensheng splurged and gave his workers eggs with their daily rice ration. Mao started working on the farm when he was six years old. But Rensheng never gave his son an extra ounce of food, and Mao was resentful about his father's unfair treatment.

PEASANT LIFE

In nineteenth-century China, most peasant children did farm chores and never went to school. Wealthier boys, whose parents dreamed of sending them to work in the imperial government under the rule of the empress, attended school and memorized the texts of Confucius, one of China's great philosophers. They also learned to read and write Chinese characters, recite Chinese history, and count on a wooden device called an abacus. Few students learned about science, geography, foreign languages, or literature.

Rensheng wanted Mao to learn enough math to manage the farm accounts. He also expected his son to be able to recite Confucian thought. Rensheng had once lost a business lawsuit to a neighbor who had brilliantly cited Confucian theory in court. Rensheng expected Mao to keep that from ever happening again.

CONFUCIANISM

onfucius (551–479 B.C.) was a unique teacher and China's first moral philosopher. For him, moral behavior was defined by traditional social roles. He believed that people must accept and live in the social class or position to which they were born. Ruler and ruled, teacher and student, parent and child, man and woman—relationships followed an expected code of behavior. Confucius's students recorded his ideas in a short text called the *Analects*, which became the base for Chinese social and political order. Literacy was measured by a person's knowledge and understanding of Confucian texts.

At the age of eight, Mao started at the village school. Relieved to get away from his father's constant commands on the farm, Mao discovered that his teacher was just as harsh. Both men believed that lazy and disobedient boys should be beaten. Mao was often their victim.

Once, when Mao was ten, he ran away from his angry teacher. Afraid that his father would punish him if he went home, Mao left his village. He wandered alone in circles for three days while his worried family searched for him. Mao's father and teacher were relieved to find the boy alive, and they tried to be nicer. Mao decided that his protest had served its purpose.

As Mao got older, he began refusing to follow his father's orders, and the two argued fiercely. Once when Rensheng criticized his son in front of guests, Mao cursed his father and stormed out of the house. Mao's parents followed him outside, and he threatened to drown himself in their lily pond. The standoff ended when Mao agreed to apologize on one bent knee (the traditional position was on two knees) if his father promised not to beat him.

"Thus the war ended," Mao later said. "And from it I learned that when I defended my rights by open rebellion, my father relented, but when I remained meek and submissive, he only cursed and beat me the more. . . . I learned to hate him."

In 1906, when Mao was thirteen, his father pulled him out of school. The family had grown, and Rensheng needed another worker in the fields. By then Wen Qimei had given birth to a third son, Zetan, and to four other babies who had all died. She had also adopted an infant girl, Zejian. Along with his siblings, Mao worked long hours on the farm. In the evening, he did the accounting and still had the energy to read until late at night. He loved tales of Chinese rebels and secret antigovernment societies.

When Mao was fourteen, his parents arranged his marriage to a twenty-year-old peasant girl known only as Miss Luo. Arranged marriages were common in China, but Mao resented being forced to wed. Miss Luo moved into the home of Mao's family, but he never considered her his wife.

In 1910 Mao left home to live with a friend. He was fed up with farm chores and wanted to study further. He borrowed money from friends and studied Confucian texts with an elderly scholar. He also borrowed books on political theory from an older cousin and began to pay attention to China's politics.

Empress Dowager Cixi, photographed here in 1903, was descended from the Manchu people of Manchuria. The Manchus had been in power since conquering China in 1644.

Chapter **TWO**

REBELLION

MANCHU EMPRESS DOWAGER CIXI RULED CHINA
from 1861 to 1908. She was part of the Manchu
dynasty, a series of rulers who belong to the same
family. She imposed unfair laws on China's peasants.
For example, the government forced peasants to pay
annual taxes in grain, which fed the imperial leaders.
When crops failed, peasants had to give up their
stored grain to pay the tax. This often left them with
nothing to eat.

The Empress Dowager faced peasant rebellion, foreign invasion, and bankruptcy. European, American,
and Japanese governments forced China into unfair
trade agreements, which strangled China's economy.
She watched as imperial power crumbled.

DESPERATE PEASANT

Meanwhile, Mao witnessed political trouble in his own province of Hunan. In the spring of 1910, peasants rioted in Changsha, the provincial capital, because of a grain shortage. The previous year, the Yangtze River had flooded its banks twice and left rice farmers homeless and without a crop. Peasants were starving.

One desperate peasant and his wife committed suicide, leaving behind three orphans. News of this double suicide reached the public and caused a peasant uprising. People demonstrated outside Changsha's government offices, but the government ignored the crisis.

Mao's father carried on his private rice trade during this unrest. When hungry villagers realized Rensheng had plenty of grain, they stole one of his rice shipments. Mao was troubled by his father's greed. But he also criticized the peasants for theft. He began to understand how little power the peasants had against wealthy merchants and an uncaring government.

Mao decided to go back to school. He enrolled in the elite Dongshan Upper Primary School in Xiangxiang, south of Shaoshan, where his uncle lived. This school offered a modern curriculum influenced by Western (European and American) educational standards. Mao persuaded his father to pay fourteen hundred copper cash (about two U.S. dollars) for five months of room, board, tuition, and books. But he found himself among classmates who snubbed him for his tattered

YELLOW CRANE TOWER

Wide, wide flow the nine streams through the land,
Dark, dark threads the line from south to north.
Blurred in the thick haze of the misty rain
Tortoise and snake hold the great river locked.

The yellow crane is gone, who knows whither?
Only this tower remains a haunt for visitors.
I pledge my wine to the surging torrent,
The tide of my heart swells with the waves.
—a poem by Mao Zedong, 1927

clothes and poor hygiene. He had trouble settling in and became depressed.

Despite his unhappiness, Mao did not cower when students challenged him. Headstrong and argumentative, he made a name for himself. Teachers noticed his writing skills, his passion for reading and writing poetry, and his love of Chinese history. He also read about such foreign leaders as the French emperor Napoleon and U.S. presidents George Washington and Abraham Lincoln. Mao finished upper primary school, and in 1911, he transferred to a secondary school in Changsha.

REPUBLICAN REVOLUTION

By 1911 many Chinese were ready to overthrow the Manchu emperor Puyi and rid themselves of the

imperial rule forever. Emperor Puyi had taken the
throne after the Empress Dowager died in 1908. The
big question was what form of government would
replace the imperial system. Some people wanted a
constitutional monarchy, in which a royal leader fol-
lows a constitution of basic laws and principles. Others wanted a full republic, a government of elected
representatives. Secret societies planned uprisings
and printed anti-Manchu pamphlets. Warlords and
their soldiers controlled certain regions of the country. But no leader was strong enough to unite China's
vast territories.

One man, Sun Yat-sen, emerged as a voice for the
republic. Sun was a doctor who had gone to mission
schools in Hong Kong and Hawaii. When he returned
to China in 1911, he found his country weak and at a
standstill. Turning to politics, Sun led uprisings
against the Manchu government and was then hunted
down and threatened with execution. Sun fled China
but continued his revolutionary activities from the
United States and Japan.

In October 1911, while Sun was fundraising in the
United States, anti-Manchu sentiment spread across
China. The population resented the Manchus and
fought to overthrow them. Over a six-week period, fif-
teen provinces withdrew from the imperial state. The
Manchus turned for help to their general, Yuan
Shikai, who had a strong army. Yuan negotiated with
the revolutionaries, and Emperor Puyi was forced to

give up his throne. Puyi and his family were allowed to remain in their palace with much of their wealth and belongings, but Manchus in other parts of China were hunted down and killed. Power struggles between the pro-Manchu upper class, independent warlords, and revolutionaries continued.

Sun Yat-sen returned to China in late December 1911 and tried to pull together the various anti-Manchu factions and secret societies. In January 1912, he founded the National People's Party, also called the Nationalist Party, or the Guomindang (Kuomintang), and became president for six weeks. But he soon realized he had no strength without an army. In February he stepped down, and General Yuan Shikai became president.

General Yuan Shikai became president of the Guomindang in 1912.

Meanshile, at his school in Changsha, Mao followed these political events in the *Minli Bao* (People's Strength) newspaper. He expressed his own political ideas through essays and discussions with friends. He also tested his rebellious nature. For example, under the Manchu government, all men had been forced to wear their hair in one long braid, a queue, which hung down the back. As a strong sign of disobedience, Mao cut off his queue and encouraged his classmates to do the same. When most of his fellow students chickened out, Mao and a friend attacked them and cut their hair.

In the early 1900s, a revolutionary soldier cut off a Chinese man's queue.

YOUNG REVOLUTIONARIES

Revolutionary soldiers soon came to Changsha to recruit young men into the army. One leader talked to students at Mao's school. Moved by the man's speech, Mao wanted to fight. But before he could enlist, revolutionary troops attacked Changsha's imperial offices. The government counterattacked and killed revolutionary leaders. The government also killed young men without queues. Mao and his short-haired friends had to hide until things settled down.

When Mao realized that the revolutionary army remained determined to overthrow imperial rule, he enlisted. Seeing very little action, he did mindless chores for the officers and wrote letters for his illiterate companions. Better educated than his fellow soldiers, Mao acted superior to them. He refused to carry his own water from the city well to the military camp. Instead, he hired a peasant to do it for him. When soldiers donated some of their pay to the revolution, Mao refused. He kept his spare money for newspapers. In the spring of 1912, he quit the army.

People gather in a public square for a temple fair in the early 1900s. After the 1912 revolution, Chinese citizens gained more freedoms than they'd had under dynastic rulers.

Chapter **THREE**

A TROUBLED REPUBLIC

UNDER THE NEW REPUBLIC, THE CHINESE EXPERIMENTED with their freedom. They opened new schools, shops, theaters, and industries. Intellectuals started newspapers and journals, and they published essays on building a new China. City people imported European and American fashions and music.

But life for the common peasant had changed little. Still powerless under landlords, business owners, and government officials, peasants also remained at the mercy of floods, droughts, and other natural disasters.

UNCLEAR FUTURE

At eighteen years old, Mao did not know what to do next. He asked his family for more money, but Rensheng refused. Mao read newspaper announcements and registered for several training programs—police academy, soap-making school, and even law school—but he wasn't set on any career. His father finally sent tuition money for business school. Mao tried this for a month and then dropped out. Instead, Mao went to the public library every day to study philosophy and poetry on his own.

Reading the *Xiang River Daily*, Mao first came across the term *Socialism*, an economic and political theory favoring government control of industry, public services, and the public distribution of goods. He read more on politics and discovered essays by Jiang Kangshu, a progressive thinker who founded the Chinese Socialist Party. It promoted the idea of "no government, no family, no religion: from each according to his ability, to each according to his need." Mao liked this idea.

In 1913 Mao finally decided to take a teacher-training program at the new Hunan Fourth Provincial Normal School in Changsha, where tuition was free. A fellow student remembered him as "a tall, clumsy, dirtily dressed young man whose shoes badly needed repairing." Easily annoyed and always ready for an argument, Mao was often plagued by self-doubt and depression. In his diary, he recorded thoughts about himself: "You do not have the capacity for tranquility. You are fickle [given to sudden changes] and excitable. Like a woman preening herself, you know no shame. Your ambitions for fame and fortune are not suppressed, and your sensual desires grow daily."

Mao was a good student when he wanted to be. He wrote strong essays, but he disliked science and art. Once, on an art exam, he drew a circle on his paper and left the room. He did not care if he failed the subjects that bored him.

Mao did like philosophy. And his philosophy teacher, Yang Changji, became his mentor. Yang often invited Mao and other students to his home to discuss new social, political, economic, and educational theories. Yang argued for equal rights for women. He was also a firm believer in the importance of physical fitness. These new ideas inspired Mao to write an article, published in April 1917 by a progressive magazine called *New Youth*.

Borrowing Yang's ideas, Mao wrote about self-improvement and the importance of exercise. He also wrote about the importance of individual will, a theme he repeated in many articles. Mao believed that each person must follow his own truth instead of blindly accepting established ideas.

STUDENT POLITICIANS

At school Mao befriended a student named Xiao Yu, who later wrote a book about their friendship. One summer vacation, Mao and Xiao Yu stayed together on campus. They enjoyed discussing philosophy, but Xiao Yu was put off by many of Mao's habits.

Mao refused to bathe, brush his teeth, or clean up his room. He gave off a terrible odor, and his teeth were covered in green film. Xiao Yu asked Mao how a great hero could save the world if he could not clean his room. Mao answered, "A great hero who thinks about cleaning up the universe has no time to think about sweeping rooms."

Mao gradually gained respect from fellow students and from his teachers. Elected president of the Students' Society, he organized community service projects. His favorite project was an evening school for local workers.

Mao and Xiao Yu formed a student group, the Xinmin Xuehui, or "New People's Study Society." The students, invited by Mao and Xiao, discussed self-improvement, strengthening moral and spiritual understanding, and social reform. In the early days, the group was not aligned with any political party, but eventually Mao began to use group meetings for radical political activities.

In June 1918, at the age of twenty-four, Mao graduated with a teaching degree. Again, he found himself without plans. That same summer, Professor Yang moved to Beijing to teach at the Beijing University. He found Mao a job in the university library.

In Beijing Mao shared a cheap room with seven other students from Changsha. In a one-story, gray-tiled house, two miles from the university, Mao, Xiao Yu, and six others slept tightly packed on a kang, a sleeping platform. They ate meager meals and debated political theories.

At work, Mao tried to talk to the famous radical thinkers who studied in the library. But nobody paid

Students study with instructors at Beijing University, where Mao worked as a library assistant. This photo was taken in 1902, before the revolution, and the students are all wearing queues. By 1919, many radical students had cut their long hair.

attention to the unknown library assistant. Mao decided that one day he would prove himself to these men.

YOUNG TROUBLEMAKER

In March 1919, Mao received a letter saying that his mother was seriously ill and would need medical treatment in Changsha for her inflamed lymph glands. Mao had already planned a trip to Shanghai with a group of students, which he did not cancel. After spending three weeks in Shanghai, Mao took a train to Changsha to see his dying mother. After she died, he decided to stay in the city.

Mao found a job teaching history part-time at a Changsha elementary school. He also met with his student group and wrote political essays. In July 1919, he started his own newspaper, the *Xiang River Review*, and called for a local reform movement in Hunan Province. On the front page of an early issue, he wrote:

> Today we must change our old attitudes.... Question the unquestionable. Dare to do the unthinkable. Religious oppression, literary oppression, political oppression, social oppression, educational oppression, economic oppression, intellectual oppression, and international oppression no longer have the slightest place in this world. All must be overthrown for the great cry of democracy.

After Mao published this article, the same Beijing intellectuals who had snubbed him in the library praised him. They said Mao had vision and persuasiveness. Mao argued strongly for educational reform, woman's rights, and anarchy, but these views soon put him in trouble with the local government. When the regional governor read Mao's essays, he closed down the newspaper. Undisturbed, Mao started writing for another newspaper. In his articles, he accused the governor of masterminding an illegal political election and of abolishing free speech. The governor retaliated by shutting down the second publication and going after Mao. To escape arrest, Mao left his teaching job and returned to Beijing to visit Professor Yang.

When Mao reached the city in January 1920, he found his mentor on his deathbed. Sick from an intestinal disorder, Yang, the man who had most inspired young Mao, died on January 17. Six days later, Mao's father died in his home village of Shaoshan.

INTRODUCTION TO COMMUNISM

While in Beijing, Mao became close friends with Professor Yang's daughter, Kaihui. They discussed current politics and read *The Communist Manifesto*. This important political text by Karl Marx and Friedrich Engels had just been translated into

Karl Marx (left) *and Friedrich Engels* (right) *wrote* The Communist Manifesto, *which introduced Mao to the ideals of Communism.*

Chinese. Mao learned the principle of class struggle from the book. During a class struggle, Marx and Engels said, the oppressed lower classes in society overthrow the ruling classes. The book also outlined the benefits of abolishing capitalism, a system that gives power and money to the middle class while laborers earn only a minimum wage, according to Marx and Engels. In the ideal Communist society, workers govern until all social classes are eliminated. At that point, people live in equal freedom and prosperity, having no further need for police or government. Mao was fascinated with Communism, as far as he understood it, and wanted to explore it further.

In April 1920, Mao went to Shanghai and took a temporary job in a laundry shop. There he spent his free time with Chen Duxiu, the editor of the *New Youth*. Mao also joined a Communist group that Chen had organized in Shanghai. In July 1920, Mao returned to Changsha and opened a bookstore and publishing company called the Cultural Book Society. His business prospered, and he hired half a dozen salespeople to run it with him. When not in the shop, Mao wrote political articles that earned him respect among the political thinkers in China. He also took a job as director of the First Hunan Primary School.

As for Mao's personal life, he made an important change in 1920. After Yang Kaihui's father died, she moved back to Changsha and met Mao again. The two fell in love and married later that year. (Mao never recognized his previous arranged marriage.) In 1921 they moved into their own house.

This portrait of Mao was taken in 1925. While Communism was taking hold in neighboring Russia, Mao hoped that a peasant revolt would lead to the spread of Communism in China.

Chapter **FOUR**

SHIFTING POLITICAL WINDS

AMID CONTINUING POLITICAL TURMOIL IN CHINA, the country was changing. Chinese business owners began using Western techniques of advertising and selling. Street lighting and telephones made cities safer and more efficient. Inflatable tires on rickshaws—small, two-wheeled vehicles pulled by one person—sped up transportation. And the return of Chinese students from study abroad brought new talent into China's industry, medicine, science, education, and public service.

Sun Yat-sen was still trying to unify his country, but he lacked the money and military strength to overthrow warlords and to bring peasant masses under central control. The Guomindang, a capitalistic government, had strong support from foreigners and wealthy Chinese. But many foreigners pocketed profits from their China-based companies and treated the Chinese like inferiors. Wealthy Chinese grew wealthier and kept their money in the family. Peasants and city laborers still worked for low wages. Mao believed that a Communist revolution could give peasants and workers more power.

COMMUNISM FROM RUSSIA

After Communist leader Vladimir Lenin took control of Russia, he tried to spread the Communist message throughout the world. To do this, he founded Comintern, the international branch of Russian Communism. In 1921 Comintern agents helped set up the first Chinese Communist Party (CCP) Congress in Shanghai. Mao attended the meeting.

Comintern agents also contacted Sun Yat-sen. They offered him money and weapons. They also advised him to combine the Guomindang and the CCP into one political force to unify China. Sun Yat-sen sent his chief of staff, Chiang Kaishek, to Moscow, Russia, to meet Lenin and study political policy and military techniques.

In 1922 Russia joined with three other neighboring republics to form the Union of Soviet Socialist Republics (USSR), also called the Soviet Union. The Soviet government was interested in building up a Communist government in China.

The following year, Mao was back in Changsha. He and two CCP colleagues, Liu Shaoqi and Li Lisan,

Sun Yat-sen (seated) *headed the Guomindang with* Chiang Kaishek (standing) *as his chief of staff. The beliefs of the capitalism-based Guomindang clashed with those of the Chinese Communist Party.*

organized labor movements to demand better conditions for workers. Mao persuaded miners to strike—to refuse to work—until employers promised better pay and safer conditions. Soon the Changsha government was after Mao again. To avoid arrest, he went to Guangzhou (Canton), where he attended the third Communist Party Congress in June. At the meeting, party members discussed the idea of joining with the Guomindang. Li Lisan was against the idea, but the majority of members, including Mao, voted for it. Also at this meeting, Mao was elected as one of nine members of the CCP Central Committee, an administrative body, and secretary of the new, five-person Central Bureau, which ran the CCP's daily affairs.

In 1923 the Guomindang and the CCP formed an uneasy partnership called the United Front. The

Guomindang supported capitalism and the CCP believed in a Communist system, so the two parties did not trust each other. However, Mao decided to work for the United Front. He traveled to Shanghai and became leader of the Guomindang Propaganda Department, which spread information about the Guomindang to the people. He also ran programs for the Guomindang Peasant Movement Training Institute, which taught peasants about politics, and edited a political publication.

THE NORTHERN EXPEDITION

In 1925 Sun Yat-sen died, leaving the Guomindang without its leader. Many Guomindang members wanted to use this time of change to get rid of the Communists and strengthen Guomindang's central control. Guomindang chief of staff Chiang Kaishek emerged as a strong leader. He betrayed Comintern advisers and allied Communists by arresting them and destroying the United Front. Chiang made this move in preparation for the July 1926 Northern Expedition. The July expedition sent Guomindang forces across China to unite the country under one authority. The Guomindang fought warlords, rival factions, and Communists. In 1927 the Guomindang killed hundreds of thousands of Communists, severely weakening the CCP. Mao lost his post in the propaganda department but continued to train peasants.

By 1928 the Guomindang controlled much of the country and had created some sense of Chinese national unity. Chiang Kaishek raised money and built a powerful army. The capital of China was moved from Beijing to Nanjing, where the Guomindang ran its central government. It modernized China's roads, established bus and tram lines in the cities, transformed the banking system, expanded the stock exchange, opened commercial airlines, and supported a promising film industry.

Meanwhile, the CCP tried to reorganize. They had formerly been against peasant involvement in political movements, but they began to realize they needed a peasant force to defeat the Guomindang. The CCP set up a peasant department in Shanghai and named Mao its leader. Mao went on a fact-finding mission through Hunan Province to record details of peasant life and eventually to form a peasant army. His mission convinced him that peasants could be a strong political force.

Giving up a normal private life for China's revolutionary cause, Mao spent little time with his family. Meanwhile, Yang Kaihui had had three sons—Anying, born in 1922, Anqing in 1923, and Anlong in 1927. They remained in Changsha when Mao traveled.

AUTUMN HARVEST UPRISING

On September 9, 1927, Mao led an uprising of peasants, coal miners, and ex-Guomindang soldiers against the Guomindang in Hunan. This ten-day battle became known as the Autumn Harvest Uprising, and it failed dramatically. Mao was captured but managed to escape and hide. But his reputation was damaged. The Chinese Communist Party removed him from all leadership positions.

Mao led about one thousand peasant soldiers in retreat to the Jinggang Mountains on the border of the Hunan and Jiangxi provinces. Over the next year, CCP generals Zhu De and Peng Dehuai marched their battered troops to Mao's camp and helped him to establish a training school and to reorganize a peasant army. Zhu De became commander of what was called the Fourth Red Army. Mao became its political chief. To inspire his soldiers and teach them battle tactics, Mao created jingles: "The enemy advances, we retreat; the enemy camps, we harass; the enemy tires, we attack; the enemy retreats, we pursue." This military instruction became a guiding principle of Mao's fighting strategies.

FOR THE LOVE OF REVOLUTION

In 1928, while still married to Kaihui, Mao fell in love with a much younger woman. He met seventeen-year-old He Zizhen in the Jinggang Mountains. She became Mao's private secretary, and Mao abandoned his wife. At the time, the marriages of CCP members were less formal than traditional marriages. Without much fanfare, He Zizhen became Mao's third wife.

To help Mao build a Communist base in the mountains, He Zizhen analyzed reports, sorted Mao's mail, gathered information from newspapers, and nursed Mao when he caught malaria. She also bore Mao a daughter in 1929 but had to give her to a peasant family when Mao moved his troops to Ruijin. He Zizhen and Mao had a son in 1932, Xiao Mao, and the three lived together for two years in Ruijin.

Meanwhile, Mao's former wife Yang Kaihui suffered a terrible fate. A warlord in Hunan arrested her because of her connection to Mao and had her beheaded. Mao's adopted sister, Zejian, was also killed. Relatives hid Mao's three older sons, but the boys were somehow taken to Shanghai and then abandoned. Living on the streets, the youngest of the three died and the middle one became mentally ill.

DISSENT IN THE PARTY

Meanwhile, CCP members disagreed about how to defeat the Guomindang. Li Lisan, then head of the CCP, wanted to carry out worker uprisings in the cities. Mao argued that Communist political policy should be adopted in small base areas in the countryside. He also argued for land reform—a method of taking property from the rich and dividing it among the peasants. He wanted peasant forces to fight in remote territories, which were harsh and unfamiliar to the Guomindang. In June 1930, the CCP adopted Li Lisan's policy. But it failed, and Li was dismissed.

Mao (standing at right) *attended a conference of representatives of peasant leagues in June 1933. Mao's vision was to motivate the peasants to form an army to challenge the Guomindang.*

Soon Mao had the chance to show the brilliance of his military tactics. The Guomindang forces tried encircling and choking off Mao's base area in Ruijin four times between December 1930 and October 1933. Each time Mao counterattacked and pushed back the Guomindang. But Chiang Kaishek's fifth encirclement campaign of more than five hundred thousand soldiers finally proved too strong for the Communists.

Mao decided to abandon Ruijin and find a safer position. Knowing how treacherous this military retreat would be, He Zizhen asked her sister to take care of two-year-old Xiao Mao until the troops settled in.

THE LONG MARCH

On the night of October 15, 1934, a yearlong Communist army retreat, called the Long March, began. Eighty-five thousand Communist soldiers, fifteen thousand CCP officials, and thirty-five women (mostly wives of the leaders) left Ruijin. Each equipped with a rifle, ammunition, a quilt, sewing materials, a mug, chopsticks, and a small portion of rice, the Communists marched, often dodging enemy fire.

For the next year, the Communists walked more than seventeen miles each day. They crossed twenty-four rivers and eighteen mountain ranges to escape the Guomindang, who were following them. Altogether the Communists covered six thousand miles of harsh landscape. At points of desperation, they ate nothing but grass, roots, and tree bark. Some walked barefoot in snow. Others suffered from malaria or typhoid fever. By the final days of the march, 95 percent of the marchers had died. Because of their sacrifice and discipline, those who survived the Long March became revolutionary heroes.

Mao and He Zizhen saw little of each other during the Long March. He Zizhen tried to do things for Mao during rest periods, but he did not notice. He had political business on his mind. He Zizhen gave birth to two more children during the march—a boy who died shortly after birth and a girl whom she left in the care of an elderly peasant woman along the way.

A Guomindang air attack seriously wounded He Zizhen. She threw herself over a soldier to protect him from gunfire and suffered a blow to the head. She was unconscious for days and had to be carried on a stretcher.

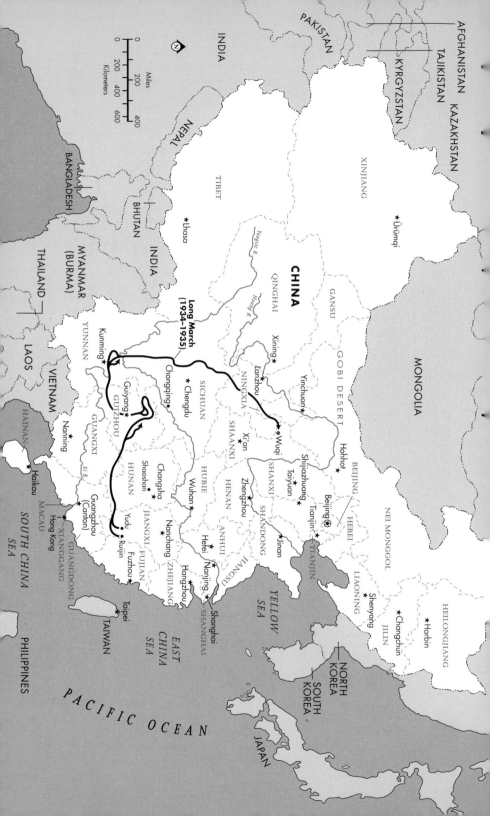

Mao (left) *and Zhou Enlai* (right) *on the Long March in this photo dated January 1935. The Communists would walk for more than a year and cover thousands of miles by the end of the journey.*

In mid-January 1935, the CCP leaders held a three-day conference at Zunyi. Because of his strong military leadership in the Long March, Mao was elected to the Politburo Standing Committee, the highest policy-making committee in the CCP. (The name of the Central Bureau had been changed to the Politburo.) As a result, he had the right to be involved in political and military decisions. General Zhu De and longtime comrade Zhou Enlai were elected to share control of the Communist military.

From left to right: *Qin Bangxian, Zhou Enlai, Zhu De, and Mao Zedong, leaders of the CCP, were stationed in the caves of Yanan in the late 1930s.*

Chapter FIVE

THE CAVES OF YANAN

IN **JANUARY 1937, THE COMMUNISTS FINALLY** reached the northern province of Shaanxi and set up headquarters in Yanan. Yanan was a trading center where villagers bargained loudly on market days. Communist soldiers, temporarily safe from the Guomindang, amused themselves in the lively town. As word went out that the Long Marchers were reorganizing in this remote region, Mao's fame as a revolutionary leader spread throughout China.

In the hillsides around Yanan were caves, which for centuries had been used as homes. Minimally furnished, without running water, electricity, or bathrooms, these caves provided simple shelter where Mao was comfortable. He believed that simple living and physical exercise benefited the individual and society. In Yanan Mao lived close to the peasants, and he talked to them whenever possible.

Under Mao's leadership, Yanan became a gathering spot for young intellectuals, writers, artists, and students who believed in the CCP's changes for China. Mao began land reform in the region and won many supporters. Every day, soldiers did military exercises. Journalists published Communist ideas, and radio announcers broadcasted CCP news to the world. The CCP provided its comrades (fellow members) with everything they needed—daily meals, three sets of clothing per year, free medical care, and education. They also taught soldiers to farm. Teams of Communist workers went into the surrounding villages and taught basic health care to the peasants. The spirit of equality and cooperation was strong, and the peasants learned to trust the Communists.

DOMESTIC BATTLES

Although Mao and He Zizhen had often been separated on the Long March, in Yanan they reestablished a home routine. He Zizhen cooked, cleaned, did secretarial tasks for Mao, and cared for their newest baby daughter, Li Min. Mao studied Communist literature, wrote essays on the struggle between social classes, and developed new political strategies.

Mao's favorite time to write or have political discussions with comrades was late at night while He

Mao (left) *sits with some of his supporters. Mao enjoyed holding political discussions late into the night.*

Zizhen slept. Soon He Zizhen felt distanced from her husband and grew jealous of the young women who flocked to Yanan and flirted with Mao.

By the spring of 1937, Mao and He Zizhen were arguing regularly. Because of their fights, He Zizhen was unhappy to learn that she was pregnant with their sixth child. She did not want to raise another baby with her disinterested husband, so she gave up on the marriage. In the autumn, He Zizhen left Yanan. She traveled to Moscow for medical treatment for her wounds from the Long March, which still bothered her. (At the time, many CCP members took advantage of Soviet health-care facilities, which were considered more modern than those in China.) In Moscow she gave birth to her last child, a boy, who died of pneumonia ten months later. Years of stress, poor nutrition, and grief over lost children (she never saw Xiao Mao or her older daughters again) finally shattered her health, and she entered a Soviet psychiatric asylum. At some point between 1940 and 1941, Mao sent his daughter, Li Min, and his two teenaged sons, Anying and Anqing (finally found in Shanghai) to Moscow to live with He Zizhen. She recovered slowly.

With his third wife gone, Mao focused on two goals. First, he sought to increase his political influence within the CCP and in China. Second, he wanted to study Marxist theory in depth and work it into his own philosophy. Mao thought China needed a form of Marxism designed especially for the Chinese people. For example, the Soviets relied on urban workers to lead the Communist movement, but Mao was creating a political force with China's peasants. "The revolutionary war is a war of the masses," Mao wrote. "It can be waged only by mobilizing the masses and relying on them."

Mao read every Marxist text that had been translated into Chinese and kept a record of his reading. He also wrote essays, defining his ideas for Chinese Communism. Two of the most important essays of Mao's Yanan days were "On Practice" and "On Contradiction." "On Practice" is about going beyond book learning and finding truth through practice. "On

"ON PRACTICE"

Discover the truth through practice, and again through practice verify and develop the truth. Start from perceptual knowledge and actively develop it into rational knowledge; then start from rational knowledge and actively guide revolutionary practice to change both the subjective and the objective world. Practice, knowledge, again practice, and again knowledge. This form repeats itself in endless cycles, and with each cycle the content of practice and knowledge rises to a higher level. Such is the whole of the dialectical-materialist theory of knowledge, and such is the dialectical-materialist theory of the unity of knowing and doing."

—Mao Zedong, 1937, from a lecture at the Anti-Japanese Military and Political College in Yanan and later published in Selected Works of Mao Tse-Tung Vol. I.

Contradiction" addresses contradictions in the laws of nature, society, and thought. Mao's ideas became famous and were known as Mao Zedong Thought.

TURBULENT GREEN WATERS

Although Mao worked long hours in Yanan, he wasted no time, at the age of forty-five, in finding a new love interest. Lan Ping, a twenty-three-year-old actress from Shanghai, caught Mao's eye at one of his lectures. The two fell in love quickly and wanted to marry.

Mao had to ask the CCP to grant him a divorce from He Zizhen. Many CCP officials still respected Mao's

In Yanan Mao met his fourth wife, Lan Ping (left), who changed her name to Jiang Qing. This photo of the two was taken in 1945.

third wife and disliked his new girlfriend. But after some argument and delay, they granted Mao's wish on one condition. Lan Ping would not be allowed to have an official CCP job. Forced to settle for being Mao's wife and personal secretary, Lan Ping resented the CCP officials who denied her a political position.

After their marriage, Lan Ping decided to give herself a revolutionary name. This was common practice among comrades. With Mao's help, she chose Jiang Qing, which means "Green Waters." Like Mao's former wives, Jiang Qing was not deeply involved in her husband's work. She spent much of her time knitting sweaters, tailoring clothing, and making the spicy food that Mao loved. In 1939 Jiang Qing gave birth to Mao's tenth child, daughter Li Na.

In public Jiang Qing was obedient, quiet, and let her husband take center stage. But in private, she was demanding, quick-tempered, and bossy. Mao confessed to a bodyguard, "I did not marry very well. I rushed into it too lightly. Jiang Qing is my wife. If she were one of my staff, I'd get rid of her as soon as I could. . . . But there's nothing I can do. I just have to put up with her."

Mao put up with Jiang Qing by ignoring her whenever possible. Before long, this marriage was as troubled as the last.

Mao makes a speech while in Yanan in the early 1940s.

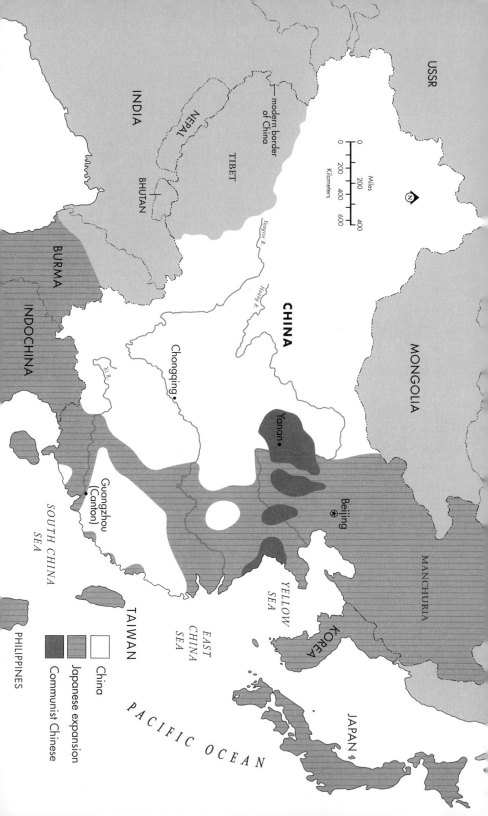

USSR

INDIA

NEPAL

modern border
of China

TIBET

BHUTAN

Yangtze R.

Hwang R.

CHINA

MONGOLIA

BURMA

INDOCHINA

XI R.

Chongqing

Yanan

Beijing

MANCHURIA

Guangzhou
(Canton)

SOUTH
CHINA
SEA

TAIWAN

YELLOW
SEA

EAST
CHINA
SEA

KOREA

PHILIPPINES

Communist Chinese
Japanese expansion
China

JAPAN

PACIFIC OCEAN

0 200 400 600
Kilometers
0 200 400
Miles

N

Chapter **SIX**

INVADERS FROM THE EAST

IN YANAN THE COMMUNISTS WORKED HARD TO strengthen their political party. Mao believed he could defeat the Guomindang and create a new society without poverty, illiteracy, forced marriage, or government corruption. But before he could do that, he had to deal with another enemy—Japan.

In the late 1930s, the Japanese invaded China's southern regions along the coast and pushed inland to the west. China declared a state of war, and World War II (1939–1945) began in Asia. The Guomindang and the CCP had to form another United Front to fight Japan. But this alliance was as unstable as the first. While fighting the Japanese, the Guomindang often launched surprise attacks on the Communists.

This weakened China's forces, which were struggling against Japan's modern army. For eight years, the Chinese people suffered bombings, starvation, torture, and rape under Japanese occupation.

World War II Allied forces—primarily France, Great Britain, the Soviet Union, and the United States—came to China's aid, but the fighting remained fierce. In August 1945, with hopes of ending World War II, the U.S. Army dropped two atomic bombs on Japan, one in Hiroshima and the other in Nagasaki. These attacks killed hundreds of thousands of Japanese and forced Japan to surrender on August 14. Japan pulled back its soldiers from all foreign territories, including China.

Mao Zedong and Chiang Kaishek each wanted to take over the regions surrendered by the Japanese. In the post World War II confusion, their weak alliance collapsed and civil war seemed certain. But Mao was afraid to attack the Guomindang first. He discovered that the Soviets had secretly signed a peace agreement with Chiang Kaishek. That meant Mao would not have Soviet Communist support in a civil war. To make matters worse, the United States also supported Chiang Kaishek. If the Communists attacked the Guomindang, they could be up against the U.S. Army.

In August 1945, Mao, who was then chairman of the Politburo and the CCP Central Committee, flew to Chongqing to meet with Chiang Kaishek and U.S. negotiators. For the next six weeks, Mao and Chiang argued over China's future government. In a written

Mao (left front) *arrived in Chongqing in September 1945 to meet with U.S. ambassador to China Major General Patrick J. Hurley* (right) *and Guomindang leader Chiang Kaishek to negotiate the future of China's government.*

treaty, Mao accepted Chiang's leadership in China. And Chiang accepted the CCP as a legitimate opposition party. They agreed not to fight a civil war, and Mao returned to Yanan.

But neither side had been honest. Even before the bargaining talks were over, Mao and Chiang Kaishek secretly planned civil war. Increasingly worried that the United States would help the Guomindang if fighting began, Mao became severely depressed.

Day after day, Mao stayed in bed, sweating, trembling, and asking for cold towels for his forehead. He could not sleep well. He asked for sleeping pills and then became addicted to them. He smoked cigarettes constantly and was unable or unwilling to act as leader. His deputy, Liu Shaoqi, stood in for him as acting head of the CCP.

Alone in his room, Mao watched China's political climate. For a time, he believed that because the United

States had called for peace between the CCP and the Guomindang, civil war could be avoided. But Mao misjudged the situation. The United States did not stop Chiang Kaishek from attacking the Communists, and the peace agreement fell apart.

CIVIL WAR

By July 1946, civil war had erupted throughout central and northern China. The fight for the motherland was on, and Mao came out of his depression. He used guerrilla warfare tactics against the Guomindang—luring tired enemy soldiers deep into unfamiliar territory and attacking them from all sides with a fresh army. "Fight no battle you are not sure of winning," Mao said.

In March 1947, the Guomindang targeted Yanan. But Mao said he was not troubled. He declared that Yanan itself was not important—he could move the CCP base. "We will give Chiang Yanan," he said. "He will give us China."

Then the Yanan bombing started. American Communist Sidney Rittenberg, who worked for Mao's radio broadcast department, remembered the frightening explosions:

> There was a brief second of silence and then the blast, which blew out the wooden door and window frames of our cave. Earth crumbled from the ceiling. We fled for the shelters and crouched down in the darkness waiting. Then the freakish

whine began again and I was suddenly seized
with a feeling of doom . . . there was an ear-split-
ting explosion, this time a direct hit on the
mountain slope just above the roof of our cave. A
section of the roof fell in, and our colleagues
from the next cave came scurrying through the
corridors of the shelter. . . . That afternoon, the
evacuation of Yanan began.

On March 18, 1947, Mao and the CCP Central Committee leaders, under military escort, abandoned Yanan.
Although his army had no foreign power behind it, Mao
was confident that he could defeat the Guomindang.
For more than twenty years, the Communists had
treated China's peasants well while the Guomindang
had done little to improve peasant life. Mao counted on
peasant support against the Guomindang.

By January 1949, the CCP controlled Tianjin and
Beijing, and the Communists kept fighting until they
had captured Shanghai and Guangzhou. In December
1949, Chiang Kaishek fled with his air force, navy,
and three hundred million dollars to the island of Taiwan. He planned to stay there until he saw a chance
to attack mainland China again.

A New World

The March 23, 1949, evening edition of the *People's
Daily* ran a headline in red ink stating: "CHAIRMAN
MAO HAS ARRIVED IN PEIPING [Beijing]." China's

Communist troops capture enemy fighters in May 1949 during the attack on Shanghai. During the civil war, Communist troops overwhelmed the Guomindang-backed forces and drove out Chiang Kaishek and his army by the end of the year.

people, so anxious about the state of their government, bought every copy of that newspaper in forty-five minutes. They were ready for peace.

On September 21, the CCP Central Committee met to name Beijing as the seat of the new central Communist government and Mao as head of state. Mao gave a moving speech:

> The Chinese people, comprising one quarter of humanity, have now stood up. The Chinese have always been a great, courageous and industrious nation; it is only in modern times that they have fallen behind . . . we have closed ranks and defeated both domestic and foreign aggressors. . . . Ours will no longer be a nation subject to insult and humiliation.

Ten days later, Mao stood before hundreds of thousands of cheering Chinese to declare the founding of the

Communist troops marched through the streets of Beijing in 1949 accompanied by a propaganda truck decorated with an image of Mao in the center of a red star, a symbol of Communism. Mao used propaganda to strengthen his popular support in China.

People's Republic of China. One Chinese writer, Maggie Huang, who grew up in the Mao era, remembers the trust people had in Mao Zedong. She said, "Mao finished with war and promised his people that the old regime was gone, and a New World had come. He was an idealist. . . . Chinese people at that time believed in him, and they loved him. They welcomed the concept of a New World."

DEEP IN THE FORBIDDEN CITY

Confident as China's new leader, Mao Zedong installed himself, his family, and the CCP Central Committee in Zhongnanhai, the former Forbidden

City. Mao's private quarters, the "Chrysanthemum Fragrance Study," surrounded a courtyard of ancient pine and cypress trees. His bedroom was large and also served as his private study. Nearby was a building with an indoor swimming pool where Mao spent much of his time swimming, eating, and resting. Surrounding him were doctors, nurses, bodyguards, and a personal attendant in charge of meals. Everything Mao ate had to pass through two laboratories, one to test for freshness and nutritional content and the other for poison.

Nearby, Jiang Qing had her own quarters. By this point, Mao and Jiang Qing had grown apart, but neither asked for a divorce. Mao simply avoided his wife and asked his staff to find him young female companions. Jiang Qing knew of her husband's infidelities but was powerless to stop them. If she made trouble, Mao could divorce her. Jiang Qing did not want to lose the special treatment she received as Mao's wife.

After years of living in military camps and Yanan caves, Mao was living like royalty. The elegant mansions within the Forbidden City—fixed up for CCP officials—indicated a great change in him. Although in his writing and speeches he still encouraged simple living, he abandoned it himself. Mao lived in a privileged world behind the same walls that had protected emperors, and he acted as if he were above the law. He was considered the great Chairman Mao. And nobody challenged him.

Mao (right) *tours Beijing in 1949, the year he declared the city the capital of the new People's Republic of China.*

Chapter **SEVEN**

REBUILDING CHINA

WHEN MAO TOOK OVER CHINA, THE COUNTRY WAS in shambles. The economy was bankrupt, and the communications and transportation systems had been destroyed. The educational and banking systems were also falling apart. Millions of people had been displaced during the civil war, and Mao wanted to improve their lives.

Within weeks of his October 1 announcements to the Chinese people, Mao traveled to the Soviet Union to meet Joseph Stalin, the Soviet Communist leader who had taken over after Lenin died in 1924. Mao respected Stalin for his strong leadership but disagreed with him on Communist policy for China. At their meetings, Stalin promised Mao credit for three hundred million U.S. dollars and offered to help China modernize.

GOVERNING A NATION

Mao began changing his country. Land reform, public education, and industrial growth were important parts of his plan. He encouraged class struggle, allowing the poor and oppressed to confront and punish the wealthy.

Class struggle was supposed to be a method for making different classes more equal. However, sometimes mobs turned deadly. China's peasants dragged landlords from their homes and tortured or killed them publicly. More than two million landlords died during China's class struggle campaigns.

CHINA'S BORDER CONFLICTS

Mao wanted to spread Communism beyond China's borders. By surrounding his country with Communist territories, he hoped to protect it from enemy attack. He knew that Chiang Kaishek wanted to regain control. Mao also worried that the United States, an anti-Communist country, might become a threat.

In 1950 Mao sent armed forces into neighboring Tibet, a country that considered itself independent. Mao declared that Tibet was a former Chinese territory and should be reunited with the Chinese motherland. He said he wanted to help Tibetan peasants through land reform and class struggle. But he really wanted to control a strategic border with India, to

A TIBETAN MONK TALKS OF MAO

n elderly Buddhist monk who fled Tibet after the Communist invasion wrote, "The destruction of Tibetan culture is due to Mao's ignorance, which blinded him to see the good things. He was so greedy to do all the things in HIS way. When people disagreed with his ideas, he killed them."

mine Tibetan minerals and gems, and to expand China's landholdings.

Tibet's Buddhist leader, the fourteenth Dalai Lama, who knew his small country was no match against the Chinese, went to Beijing to negotiate peace with Mao. Despite his efforts, the Dalai Lama could not find a peaceful solution, and years of fighting followed. The Dalai Lama escaped into exile in India, and one hundred thousand Tibetans followed him out of their homeland. The Communists quickly crushed Tibet's government, replaced its ancient cultural practices with Chinese Communist policies, and killed more than one million Tibetans.

Mao also sent his army into Xinjiang, an ethnically mixed territory on the Soviet border. Although this region had been largely independent of Beijing's authority since 1911, Mao wanted control of it. China needed Xinjiang's oil, coal, and minerals. The Communists built a railroad system to transport Xinjiang's products to central China. As Mao had done in Tibet, he sent Chinese citizens and troops into Xinjiang to control the region. This action resulted in many violent clashes between the Chinese and Xinjiang's Uyghur people, a Turkic Muslim group. Like the Tibetans, many Uyghurs escaped the violence and resettled outside of their homeland.

Mao also had trouble on his eastern border. Communist North Korea, supported by Soviet Communists, invaded non-Communist South Korea in 1950. In response, the United States sent troops to help South Korea, and the Korean War (1950–1953) began. Fearing that the United States would take control of North Korea, Mao sent soldiers, including his son

U.S. Marines captured Chinese Communist soldiers in central Korea during the Korean War. Chinese troops often attacked U.S. forces at night and wore North Korean uniforms to avoid directly provoking the United States into a war with China.

Mao Anying, to push the United States southward. The Korean War took the lives of more than 148,000 Chinese soldiers, including that of Mao's son. When Mao heard that his son had died, he grew silent. Trembling so much that he could not light his cigarette, he resolutely announced, "In revolutionary war, you always pay a price. Anying was one of thousands." For Mao death was an inevitable part of a Communist revolution. As long as the goal was correct, as long as Communism benefited the masses, violence was justified. "A revolution is not a dinner party," Mao said. "A revolution is an insurrection . . . an act of violence by which one class overthrows another."

COUNTERREVOLUTIONARIES

After the CCP took over in China, millions of Guomindang supporters remained in their homeland. A few acted as spies and agents for the Guomindang in Taiwan, which wanted to regain power in China. Mao and the CCP launched a program, called a campaign, to identify China's counterrevolutionaries—Guomindang supporters and people who opposed Communist policy. Workers began to denounce their bosses as counterrevolutionaries. Villagers denounced neighbors. Sometimes family members denounced one another. Nobody knew whom to trust.

Many victims were innocent, but the campaign became brutal. Hundreds of thousands of counterrevolutionaries suffered humiliation, torture, forced labor, or even death.

THE THREE ANTIS AND FIVE ANTIS CAMPAIGNS

Even before the counterrevolutionary campaign was over, Mao launched several new campaigns. In 1951 his Three Antis program (anticorruption, antiwaste, and antibureaucratism) was meant to identify corruption in the CCP and in business administration. Mao targeted three groups of people: corrupt CCP members, administrative officials, and managers of factories and other businesses. People were encouraged to attack senior officials who had taken bribes or used their positions for personal power.

Mao also launched the Five Antis campaign (antibribery, antitax evasion, antifraud, antiembezzlement, and antileakage of state secrets). This program targeted middle-class capitalists working in business. The CCP taught workers how to look into their employers' business affairs to find tax evasion or other corruption. The CCP encouraged businesspeople to denounce (speak out against) one another and told citizens to write letters denouncing businesses. Business leaders had to go through public criticism sessions to confess their past business crimes. The CCP forced family members and friends to join the attack. Few of the Three Antis and Five Antis victims were killed, but they were humiliated and forced to pay fines for their crimes. The CCP took away property from some and sent others to labor camps. The main goal of the CCP's campaigns was to assert control from the top level of government down to the private home.

MAO'S FIVE-YEAR PLAN

In 1953 Mao began a Five-Year Plan for strengthening Communism throughout China. He ordered a three-stage approach for a government takeover of all private business and property. The first stage was creating mutual aid teams of villagers who shared tools and animals and worked the land as a group. The second stage was primary stage cooperatives. The government paid villagers according to how much land they made public and how hard they worked. The final stage was called advanced stage cooperatives. All land, tools, and farm animals belonged to the local government.

Mao's plan did not go well at first, and it caused debate among China's leaders. Finance Minster Bo Yibo disagreed with the fast pace of adopting Communism. Many peasants who had just gained land from the wealthy did not want to give it up. The cooperative plan also confused peasants who had just begun making a profit. The policies resulted in village debt and grain shortage, but Mao paid no attention to setbacks and objections. He pushed Communism forward.

Mao's Five-Year Plan also involved industry. Because China had few factories, Mao turned again to the Soviet Union for help. The Soviets sent experts and money to set up steel factories in China. Many Chinese students went to the Soviet Union to learn about engineering, steel manufacturing, and transportation technology. China's steel production soon increased from 174,000 tons to 6 million tons per year. China also had laid down over twenty-seven thousand miles of railroad tracks across the country. The expanded transportation system allowed the government to move large numbers of people and products around the country more easily than ever before.

Mao was confident that his policies were good for China. But he looked at the Soviet Union and grew nervous about the political rebellions going on there. Nikita Khrushchev came to power after Joseph Stalin died, and he publicly criticized Stalin's policies. Mao feared the same thing could happen to him. He began to distrust the people around him.

ONE HUNDRED FLOWERS MOVEMENT

In 1956 Mao began a new movement to encourage political debate. Wanting to know what people thought of China's progress, he started the One Hundred Flowers Movement. He asked people to express their political opinions honestly. But who would dare? After witnessing the violence against counterrevolutionaries, most people were afraid to talk about politics.

But Mao promised that the political debate would be safe. Eventually, students and teachers began to hang posters containing political comments on what was called the Democracy Wall at Beijing University. Gradually people started criticizing the CCP. They complained that CCP members acted like bureaucrats, people who enforced rigid policies. Intellectuals complained about censorship in the arts.

Mao was unprepared for such widespread discontent. At first, Mao listened to the criticism and made no reply. Then, as the criticism became more intense, Mao grew angry. In June 1957, he broke his promise of a safe debate and claimed that he had launched the One Hundred Flowers Movement to identify "poisonous weeds," people who opposed Communism. Those who had voiced opposition to Communist policy were labeled rightists. Mao wanted all rightists rounded up and punished. He called this his Antirightist Movement.

Mao asked Deng Xiaoping, the newly appointed CCP secretary-general, to do the brutal job. The central government ordered all offices and organizations to identify a certain number of rightists in their groups. If nobody qualified, the offices named innocent people to reach the required number, or quota. Torn from job and family, rightists went to labor camps or jail for years. Some died, and others suffered mental breakdowns.

In one quick movement, China silenced its best scientists, engineers, teachers, and artists. The campaign often left unqualified people to run China's industries, engineering projects, schools and colleges, and arts programs. But Mao kept his trust in the Chinese peasants. They would save China.

THE GREAT LEAP FORWARD

After the horror of the Antirightist Movement, Mao did not let China settle down. Revolution was an ongoing process for him. In the autumn of 1957, he talked boldly of starting an industrial and agricultural revolution. He called his new plan the Great Leap Forward.

Increased steel production was Mao's big goal. He hoped to overtake Great Britain in the production of steel. He wanted regional leaders to set up small, backyard furnaces for steelmaking. Villagers donated pots, pans, and cooking utensils that could be melted for steel. Trees were cut down for furnace fuel. Peasants who normally tended field crops worked at the furnaces. In the end, the peasant effort was tremendous, but the steel was unusable. And crops died from neglect.

During the Great Leap Forward, grain production was also supposed to increase. Instead of one harvest per year, Mao wanted two. To bring about this increase, China opened large communes, or shared areas, where up to forty thousand people lived together. Family life was discouraged so people could put all their effort into field labor. Children reared in communal nurseries, and the elderly moved into supervised homes.

Mao also wanted to get rid of China's pests. He told the people to kill insects and pesky sparrows furiously. Then he ordered people to gather thousands of dead birds in a pile to prove the people's dedication to the Great Leap Forward. There was one major problem

As part of Mao's Great Leap Forward, Chinese workers operate backyard blast furnaces to melt steel from everyday metal items.

with this plan. With the sparrows gone, the insects had no enemy. The insect population increased and devoured the meager crops left in the fields.

When Mao toured the countryside in 1958 to see the results of his agricultural revolution, he was fooled. Regional leaders exaggerated production figures and pretended to be enthusiastic about the Great Leap Forward. Fearing the rightist label, nobody wanted to tell Chairman Mao that his expectations were unreasonable.

Sidney Rittenberg, the American Communist who worked for the CCP, summed up Mao's error in the Great Leap Forward: "Mao's cardinal problem was that he always wanted to move faster than what was possible. He wanted to show the world he really was concerned for country people. He enjoyed seeing them better off. But he thought that he could get to full Communism before the Russians. That was an idea that he cherished."

The Great Leap Forward ended in disaster. Because regional leaders had overestimated crop production, the state taxed the communes at a high rate and took more grain than the peasants could afford to give up. Over the next two years, between twenty and thirty million peasants died of famine while China exported grain. And the country suffered a severe economic depression.

QUESTIONING MAO

One party official was brave enough to question Mao's Great Leap policies. At a 1959 CCP meeting at Lushan, a mountain town in Jiangxi Province, Minister of Defense Peng Dehuai wrote Mao a private letter challenging his policies. A former Long Marcher, like Mao, and a commander in the Korean War, Peng was careful not to blame Mao alone. But he said too much.

Mao was angry. He copied Peng's letter and distributed it to CCP leaders at the meeting. Then he criticized Peng openly. Although many CCP members agreed with Peng Dehuai, they knew better than to say so. Top officials Zhou Enlai, Liu Shaoqi, and Deng Xiaoping all publicly sided with their chairman.

During the political confusion at the meeting, Jiang Qing, Mao's wife, made an unexpected move and showed up to support Mao. Although the Politburo had denied her a role in politics, they did not stop her from supporting her husband at Lushan. "I rushed here because I was worried about the chairman," Jiang Qing declared.

But Jiang Qing had hidden motives for going to Mao's side. For many years, she had wanted political power, and she saw a chance to get it. She also wanted Mao's attention. She plotted and schemed with him to make Peng Dehuai look like a rightist and Mao like China's savior. By helping her husband, Jiang Qing regained his trust and showed herself as a true revolutionary.

Mao and Jiang Qing's plan succeeded. The CCP's Central Committee dismissed Peng Dehuai and replaced him with Lin Biao, a Mao loyalist. To prove Peng Dehuai wrong, Mao continued with his Great Leap Forward plans. But terrible floods in south China and droughts in north China resulted in poor harvests again. The famine worsened, and peasants resented commune life and the destruction of family. Mao's policies had to change.

Because Peng Dehuai disagreed with Mao's approach to agricultural production in the Great Leap Forward, he was dismissed for his disloyalty to the chairman.

In October 1959, Soviet leader Nikita Khrushchev (right) attended a party in Beijing in honor of the tenth anniversary of the founding of the People's Republic of China. Although the Soviets had backed the establishment of Communism in China ten years earlier, tension between the two governments was beginning to show by this time.

Chapter **EIGHT**

BEHIND CLOSED DOORS

AFTER THE GREAT LEAP FORWARD AND THE LUSHAN conference, Mao had to slow the pace of Communist reform. In an act of self-criticism, he gave up his position as chairman of the People's Republic but kept his role as CCP chairman. Liu Shaoqi took over running the central government, and Deng Xiaoping and Zhou Enlai worked with him.

Threatened by criticism, Mao became depressed again. At the same time, his relations with Soviet leader Khrushchev broke down. Khrushchev disapproved of China's massive commune system, and Mao accused the Soviet leader of abandoning Marxism. After two visits to China, Khrushchev withdrew Soviet technicians and stopped sending financial aid to the country.

Although Liu Shaoqi was in power, Mao still saw himself as China's supreme chief and the most important Communist leader. He expected to be consulted for major political decisions. He soon began to complain that Liu and Deng treated him like a dead ancestor and were leading China away from Communism.

Despite Mao's grumbling, Liu and Deng saw positive results from their reforms. For example, they reduced the size of rural communes and returned some individual farms to the peasants. This change improved China's economy, and food became more available. Private markets reopened in the villages, and the government started new industrial, agricultural, and educational programs. China was stabilizing at last. But Mao did not like Liu's methods of allowing private businesses. Mao began to think that it was time for another revolution.

Mao's Inner Circle

According to Mao's personal physician, Dr. Li Zhisui, Mao's inner circle—known as Group One—was a web of blackmail and corruption. Plotting his return to frontline politics, Mao watched the people around him closely. His favorite bodyguards and female companions advised him on whom to trust or distrust. Mao also talked to his regional CCP leaders outside Beijing to determine if they supported him.

Mao was good at hiding his political intentions. The people who served him tried frantically to figure out

MAO'S NUCLEAR POWER

On August 22, 1964, Mao met with a group of international delegates stopping over in Beijing after a peace conference in Japan. He talked to them about nuclear weapons defense. He said, "Most of you seated here represent countries which, like us, have no atomic bombs. In dealing with U.S. aggression, we have a common interest, not only among our friends here, but with the entire world. The world cannot avoid changes; those who engage in unpopular activities of aggression will suffer defeat . . . on the question of opposing imperialism and particularly US imperialism we all stand together."

What Mao did not say was that China's team of nuclear scientists had tested three atomic bombs one week before this meeting. When he announced China's nuclear bomb success at a CCP meeting, comrades applauded him enthusiastically. The government made the following statement about using nuclear bombs. "China is developing nuclear weapons not because it believes in their omnipotence nor because it plans to use them. On the contrary, in developing nuclear weapons, China's aim is to break the nuclear monopoly of the nuclear powers and to eliminate nuclear weapons."

his plans. They bugged Mao's sleeping quarters on his train and in the guesthouses where he stayed. When one of Mao's mistresses learned of the bugging and told Mao, he was furious. He did not want details of his private life discussed outside Group One. More important, he did not want China's central government to know what he said to regional CCP leaders. Mao punished the staff members who were involved in the bugging and grew even more suspicious of those around him.

THE GREAT PROLETARIAN CULTURAL REVOLUTION

To signal his return as China's great leader, the seventy-two-year-old Mao pulled a publicity stunt. On July 16, 1966, in front of many cameras, Mao plunged into the Yangtze River and swam for more than an hour. The next day, the Chinese people opened their

To dispel rumors of failing health, Mao (bottom) *swam with some attendants in the Yangtze River in July 1966.*

newspapers and saw photos of the chairman looking as vigorous as ever. Mao, the revolutionary hero, was back in control.

Next, to launch his Great Proletarian (working class) Cultural Revolution, Mao chose Lin Biao to be his right-hand man. Putting aside problems with his wife, Mao also worked with Jiang Qing because she had close friends in Shanghai, China's cultural center. Mao decided that this revolution would start as an attack on intellectuals in the arts and in education. He used Shanghai as his power base to challenge Liu Shaoqi and Deng Xiaoping.

For his part in Mao's plan, Lin Biao, head of the People's Liberation Army, created a Cult of Mao. Lin ordered radio stations to mention Mao's name often and demanded that images of Mao be hung throughout China. Lin encouraged soldiers and citizens to read Mao's book called *Quotations from Chairman Mao Zedong*. Soon people were quoting Mao in the streets, and the publicity helped Mao's popularity.

Jiang Qing's role was to gather radical supporters into a revolutionary cultural force. Her group's purposes were to eliminate intellectuals who opposed Communist revolution and to fill new art, theater, and film with Mao Zedong Thought. Jiang Qing and her three closest comrades, whom Mao called the Gang of Four, went at their job with intensity. Anyone who had ever stepped on Jiang Qing's toes in the past became her victim.

A GUOMINDANG GENERAL IN COMMUNIST CHINA

Hanmin Wu was a Guomindang general and a business owner. He owned flour, textile, and match factories in Quzhou, and he lived in an expensive home. When the Chinese Communist Party (CCP) gained control of China, Hanmin Wu escaped with other Guomindang leaders to Taiwan. He had to leave his family in China.

In the early 1950s, the CCP wanted to expand China's industry. They encouraged Wu to return and open new factories. Wu came back and used his own money to open milk and sweater factories and a department store. At first, the Communists did not interfere with his successful businesses.

During Mao's One Hundred Flowers Movement (1956–1957), Wu joined others and offered criticism of CCP policy. Later, in the antirightist movement when Mao turned against his critics, Wu was arrested. He was charged as a counterrevolutionary and jailed. The CCP seized Wu's businesses, and he spent three years in jail.

In 1966, during the Cultural Revolution, Red Guards attacked Wu's family. They stormed into Wu's home and confiscated all the furniture but two beds. Red Guards forced Wu's mother, a Buddhist, into a public struggle session. They made her wear a dunce cap and took away her prayer beads. Upset and humiliated, she later committed suicide by jumping from a window. The Red Guards also tortured and jailed Wu's son. The young man could have won his freedom if he had denounced his father, but he refused. At one point, he was kept in solitary confinement for forty-five days. Wu's son later said of Mao, "Mao's greatness was not from doing a lot of good things for people but from making big changes. Mao disrupted the world."

Going back to Beijing and regaining control of the CCP's Central Committee, Mao called on China's youths to join his revolution. "To rebel is justified," Mao announced to the Chinese people. And what an explosion those words caused!

By September 1966, millions of students flocked to Beijing to join the movement. They put on red armbands and called themselves Red Guards. From Beijing Red Guards hopped trains—Mao allowed them free travel—and spread revolution to every corner of China. They took Mao's ideals and attacked people who adhered to the Four Olds—old thought, old culture, old customs, and old habits. The Four Olds represented China before Communism and had no place in Mao's new China.

Red Guards brought violence to China's villages. They smashed old temples, took control of CCP offices, and fought with former landowners. In street fighting alone, tens of thousands of citizens died. Red Guards marched into private homes and searched for antiques, paintings, photo albums, religious icons, foreign books, foreign music, and foreign clothing—anything that connected people to traditional or foreign culture. If Red Guards caught someone with these items, they dragged the person into the streets for public humiliation and beatings. These public events were called struggle sessions, and people feared them. Desperate to escape the Red Guards, thousands of Chinese committed suicide.

In Tibet the Cultural Revolution destroyed what was left of Tibetan culture. Red Guards tore monasteries apart, burned holy texts, broke statues, shredded religious paintings, and outlawed pictures of the Dalai Lama. Many Tibetans who had not left their country in 1959 tried to flee into exile.

Alarmed by Red Guard violence, Liu Shaoqi and Deng Xiaoping tried to stop it. But Mao made the two leaders his next targets. Jiang Qing, who disliked both Liu and Deng, encouraged the Red Guards to write articles against them. And she criticized them at CCP meetings.

Red Guards forced their way into Liu and Deng's homes. They beat Liu and dragged him off to prison. There he died alone of pneumonia. Mao took away Deng's government titles and sent him and his family to live under house arrest in Jiangxi Province. Deng was not allowed to leave his home except to work in a tractor repair shop during the day.

Beginning in the spring of 1967, China was in turmoil. Schools and regional government offices shut down, and industrial progress stopped. The people were frightened. Losing control of their own movement, Red Guards splintered into different groups and fought each other, sometimes until death. Finally, Mao's government took action to restore calm. The People's Liberation Army marched into cities, took control from the Red Guards, and reestablished a sense of order.

GOVERNMENT SHUFFLE

After Mao removed Liu Shaoqi and Deng Xiaoping from office, he was not sure whom to name as his political successor. Zhou Enlai, the only top official who had survived more than fifty years of political upheaval, was serving as China's premier. But by the late 1960s, he had cancer and was too frail to take over after Mao.

Jiang Qing and her radical group had gained power in the CCP Politburo, and she wanted to be China's next chairman of the People's Republic (the top government position Mao had abandoned after the Lushan conference). But Mao blocked her. He knew she had made too many enemies during the Cultural Revolution.

Lin Biao appeared to be a good choice. He had promoted Mao's leadership, and he controlled branches of the military. But tension grew between the two men. Mao knew that Lin wanted the position of chairman, but Mao was against it. He suspected that Lin wanted to assassinate him. In the fall of 1971, his suspicions were confirmed. After returning from a trip south, Mao learned that Lin Biao's son, Lin Liguo, had plotted to assassinate him and set up an opposition government with his father as leader. One of Lin Liguo's plans, which was not carefully organized or carried out, was to blow up Mao's Group One train. Historians argue about how much Lin Biao knew of his son's plans. But after Mao found out, Lin Liguo feared for his life. He fled China with his father and mother in an air force jet. The circumstances of this escape attempt are not clear. But Lin Biao and his family never made it to safety. Their plane crashed inside the Mongolian border, and all the passengers died.

Red Guards line up in front of a portrait of Mao in Beijing in the late 1960s. Mao's picture could be seen at important events and places throughout China as part of the Cultural Revolution.

Chapter **NINE**

COMRADES FALLING

MAO CLAIMED THAT LIN BIAO HAD BETRAYED HIM and he used the claim to discredit Lin. At the same time, Mao's fear of assassination increased. He became depressed again and was unable to sleep. He also suffered from high blood pressure, swelling in his lower limbs, lung congestion, and an irregular heartbeat. Dr. Li recommended antibiotic shots to clear Mao's lungs, but Mao refused treatment. He stayed in bed for two months, but his mind wasn't at rest. He was trying to decide on a new plan for his government.

Mao did not know whether to encourage more radical rebellion or restore moderation in the government. The radicals, led by Jiang Qing and her Gang of Four, and the moderates, represented by Zhou Enlai, both wanted Mao's attention and support. They were waiting to take over the government after Mao died.

But Mao was determined to make one more political move. He surprised his radical comrades when he reopened diplomatic relations with the United States, relations that had been closed since 1949. In April 1971, Mao invited the U.S. Ping-Pong team to Beijing. Zhou Enlai greeted the U.S. athletes in the Great Hall of the People and announced a new friendship between China and the United States. Three months later, secret talks between U.S. national security adviser Henry Kissinger and Zhou Enlai began. The two arranged for President Richard Nixon to visit China in February 1972.

Three weeks before Nixon's arrival, Mao was very sick but refused medicine. Then he decided he wanted to impress President Nixon, and he asked Dr. Li to treat him. Examining Mao, Dr. Li diagnosed heart trouble. He also saw that Mao had a serious disorder of the central nervous system (which was later identified as Lou Gehrig's disease). Mao's speech was slurred, and he was at risk for a major heart attack. He finally agreed to take medicine, and he practiced getting up from a chair and walking to strengthen his weak legs.

On February 21, 1972, Nixon arrived at the Beijing airport on Air Force One, the U.S. president's official plane. Zhou Enlai met him. Mao sent word that he wanted to meet Nixon right away, so the U.S. president jumped into a limousine and sped off to Zhongnanhai where Mao was waiting impatiently in his study.

On a momentous occasion, Mao (left) *shakes hands with U.S. president Richard Nixon* (right) *in February 1972. It was the first visit ever by a U.S. president to China.*

Dressed in a new suit, aided by his favorite female attendant, Zhang Yufeng, Mao stood to shake hands as Nixon entered his reception room. Holding Nixon's hand in both of his for a moment, Mao recognized the importance of the event. Here stood the supreme leader of China's Communist Party shaking hands with the leader of the most powerful capitalist country in the world. The two men represented opposing beliefs, but they agreed to encourage good relations between their countries.

SETTLING SUCCESSION

After Nixon's visit, Mao wanted to decide who would succeed him as China's leader. He had made unwise choices in his last two political successors—Liu Shaoqi and Lin Biao. In doing so, he had lost the confidence of the Chinese people. The country needed a solid government and an end to chaos. But Mao wanted to die knowing that the Chinese Communist revolution would continue.

In February 1973, Mao made another surprise move that angered Jiang Qing and her radical partners. Mao called Deng Xiaoping back from political exile. Deng had written Mao twice, admitting his past errors and asking Mao if he could serve the revolution again. Mao appointed Deng as one of several vice premiers under Zhou Enlai. Back in government, Deng helped restore China's agriculture, industry, defense, science, and technology.

But Deng ignored radical tactics and class struggle, and this angered Jiang Qing and her Gang of Four. She saw herself as China's next revolutionary hero, and she was not going to let Deng Xiaoping get in her way. Jiang Qing openly criticized Deng again during Politburo meetings and plotted to bring him down.

MOURNING A LOST HERO

On January 8, 1976, Zhou Enlai died of cancer. Because he had been one of China's most popular heroes, more than a million people lined the streets of

Beijing to see his funeral procession. Bedridden, Mao did not attend the funeral. And he would not allow the staff of Zhongnanhai to wear black armbands as a sign of mourning. Some say he resented the public's affection for Zhou.

Two months later, to celebrate the upcoming Qingming, the "Festival of the Dead," the people of Beijing left wreaths of mourning for Zhou Enlai at the Monument to the People's Heroes in Tiananmen Square. The movement started spontaneously, but each day the crowds grew larger. People made speeches, sang, composed poetry, and put up political posters around the square. And then they started to criticize Jiang Qing and her radical group and to defend Deng Xiaoping as China's great modernizer.

On April 4, 1976, the actual day of Qingming, the crowds swelled to hundreds of thousands. Too sick to witness the event, Mao relied on secondhand reports. The political demonstrations upset Jiang Qing and the Gang of Four. They called an emergency Politburo meeting and told members that the demonstration was a counterrevolutionary movement. The government ordered all wreaths, banners, and posters to be removed from the square.

On April 5, crowds returned to the empty monument and grew angry and loud. The Politburo sent in the militia to arrest resisters. Jiang Qing, who stood at a window in the Great Hall of the People, watched through binoculars. After the military cleared the square, she hurried to report to Mao. At a feast that evening, Jiang Qing announced, "We are victorious . . . I will become a bludgeon, ready to strike."

And strike she did. She blamed Deng Xiaoping for the demonstrations, and the government punished him again by taking away all his former titles. Fearing for his life, Deng sought refuge with a military general in the southern Guangdong Province. There, he waited to see how the government shifted over the next few months.

As China's politics heated up, Mao's health got worse. He lost weight and began drooling. His eyesight clouded over, and he suffered from paralysis on his right side. He also had difficulty speaking, and only Zhang Yufeng understood him. But Mao still had to choose a successor. He stunned the CCP and the country by choosing a man whom few people knew.

Hua Guofeng was an unlikely candidate for number one leader, but Mao liked this moderate vice premier. In a scribbled message dated April 30, 1976, Mao wrote to Hua, "With you in charge, I am at ease."

Predictably, Jiang Qing and her gang disliked Mao's choice. Until Mao was gone, they had to restrain themselves. But secretly, Jiang Qing planned to topple Hua Guofeng.

GRADUAL DECLINE

On May 11, 1976, one of Mao's nurses ran for Dr. Li. In his private study, Mao was sweating profusely and gasp-

Jiang Qing, Mao's fourth wife, became a powerful political figure during Mao's last years.

ing for air. He had suffered a heart attack and needed emergency medical treatment. Dr. Li told Hua Guofeng about Mao's failing health, and Hua met with the Politburo to prepare for Mao's death. Four leaders, including Hua Guofeng, oversaw Mao's medical treatment.

During the next few weeks, Mao's poor health made him irritable and restless. Too sick to get up on his own, he called attendants to move him from his bed to a sofa and then back to his bed. He refused blood tests, and his doctors could not track his medical complications.

Jiang Qing made matters worse. She insisted on massaging Mao when he was supposed to be resting. Once she had him rolled onto his right side, which caused him to stop breathing. Mao turned blue, and doctors had to revive him quickly. Some of Mao's staff thought Jiang Qing was trying to kill Mao.

Chairman Mao's body lay in state on September 12, 1976, as mourners passed by. His body was draped with a flag bearing the hammer and sickle—two symbols of Communism.

After Mao suffered another heart attack on June 26, Dr. Li called in twenty-four nurses and fifteen doctors to watch Mao around the clock.

THE END OF AN ERA

On September 9, 1976, surrounded by attendants, medical staff, and Politburo members, Mao Zedong died while grasping his doctor's hand. He was eighty-three. The Chinese people were shocked by the news. They had not known how sick Mao had been. After his death, they worried about government change.

For the next several weeks, outdoor radio speakers announced Mao's death to all of China. Newspapers published Mao's photo and writings. Expressions of sympathy arrived from around the world, and the Chinese people struggled to understand what Mao's death meant for their country.

As expected, a power struggle erupted. Hua Guofeng

took over as Mao had ordered. He arranged Mao's funeral. He also called Politburo meetings to keep the government running. But political groups threatened one another for central control, and tension mounted in Zhongnanhai.

Hua Guofeng learned that Jiang Qing and Mao's nephew, Mao Yuanxin, were plotting to take over the government. Hua arrested them along with the three other members of Jiang Qing's gang. Put into solitary confinement, Jiang Qing never saw freedom again. Suffering from cancer, she eventually committed suicide.

Deng Xiaoping returned to Beijing and took political power away from Hua Guofeng. In July 1977, the Tenth Party Congress reinstated all of Deng's former titles. Deng quickly established a new economic policy. He wanted to modernize China and open up trade with the United States—a policy that went against Mao's revolutionary ideals. Deng also allowed people to go to school for a career of their own choosing, start their own businesses, and choose their own marriage partners. Instead of rising up against Deng, China's people applauded the new freedoms he allowed. They had had enough of Mao's radical policies and violent disruption.

Mao Zedong's life and reputation cannot be summed up in one simple sentence. Nor should the man be denied his place in history. Defined by contradictions, moved to change the world, Mao Zedong was a flawed, complicated, but powerful leader.

EPILOGUE

Mao Zedong was China's best-known twentieth-century revolutionary leader. As philosopher, poet, and military man, he saved China from foreign oppression and challenged the power of the Manchu dynasty and the wealthy class. He gave land to struggling peasants, educated them, and raised the social position of women.

However, after Mao turned from revolutionary commander to China's chairman, he failed on many accounts. He contradicted his own policies, and his radical movements led to economic disaster, political and religious intolerance, starvation, violence, and terror.

Since Mao's death in 1976, scholars have debated his theories and his personality. Mao's doctor has revealed aspects of his lifestyle—particularly his love affairs and depressions—that shocked many. Some historians claim that Mao was mentally ill. Others say he suffered from an early onset of senility, the loss of his mental faculties. These modern diagnoses were made by looking back at Mao's behavior: his need to control people, his distrust of others, his sensitivity to criticism, and his inability to form long-lasting friendships. Mao was a neglectful husband to each of his four wives and an absent father of ten children. He was a man of politics, and his personal life was secondary.

Who was Mao? Should he be judged by the same measure as any person? Or should revolutionary leaders be judged differently? To understand Mao, you must first understand China's history and then examine his role in it. In Mao's life story, the two cannot be separated.

MAO: FACT OR FICTION

Uncovering the facts of Mao Zedong's life is a challenge. Mao liked to tell his own version of history, and portray himself in the best light. He often hid his political motives and his personal life. The Chinese Communist Party has promoted whatever version of Mao's life best suited their political purpose. The party limits access to Mao's papers and punishes anyone who reveals government secrets.

Historians and biographers differ in their accounts of Mao's life. In their books, historian Philip Short and former CCP member Sidney Rittenberg portray young Mao as a popular leader of China's peasants and a military strategist in the Communist Long March. They write that Mao and the Red Army won China's civil war without significant foreign aid. In contrast, coauthors Jung Chang and Jon Halliday claim that Mao cared little for China's peasants, that he showed no military brilliance during the Long March, and that he could not have won the civil war without Soviet aid. Short and Rittenberg show many sides to Mao. Chang and Halliday present Mao as little more than a ruthless murderer and half-hearted Communist.

Historians and biographers will continue to argue about who Mao was and what he did until all the facts of Mao's life are revealed.

CHRONOLOGY OF MAO'S LIFE

1893 Mao is born on December 26.

1911 The overthrow of the Manchu emperor takes place.

1912 Sun Yat-sen establishes the National People's Party, and Mao joins the revolutionary army.

1913 Mao begins Hunan Fourth Provincial Normal School.

1918 Mao works at Beijing University library.

1920 Mao becomes elementary school head and marries Yang Kaihui.

1921 Mao attends the first Congress of the Chinese Communist Party (CCP).

1923–27 Mao works in the United Front of the Guomindang and the CCP.

1927 Mao leads the Autumn Harvest Uprising and retreat to Jinggangshan.

1928 Mao and He Zizhen start living together.

1934 The Long March begins.

1935 Mao attends the Zunyi conference and gains strength in the CCP.

1937–45 Mao commands Communist forces during China's war with Japan.

1938 Mao marries Jiang Qing.

1945 The U.S. drops two atomic bombs on Japan ending World War II in Asia. Mao negotiates peace with Chiang Kaishek.

1946–49 Mao commands Communist troops during China's civil war.

1949 Mao announces the establishment of the People's Republic of China.

1950 The Korean War begins.

1953 Mao launches his Five-Year Plan for agriculture and industry.

1956–57 Mao carries out the One Hundred Flowers Movement.

1957 Mao launches an attack against critics in his Antirightist Movement.

1958–60 Mao carries out the Great Leap Forward.

1959 Peng Dehuai challenges Mao at the Lushan conference.

1966 Mao and Jiang Qing start the Cultural Revolution.

1967 Mao attacks CCP leaders Liu Shaoqi and Deng Xiaoping.

1969 Mao names Lin Biao as his successor.

1971 Mao learns that Lin Biao plotted to assassinate him.

1972 Mao meets U.S. president Richard Nixon in Beijing.

1973 Mao allows Deng Xiaoping back into the government.

1976 CCP leader Zhou Enlai dies, and Mao limits public mourning. Mao names Hua Guofeng as his successor. Mao dies on September 9.

GLOSSARY

anarchy: a political theory that holds that all forms of governmental authority are unnecessary and that society is based on voluntary cooperation of individuals or groups

capitalism: an economic system characterized by private ownership of property and by prices, production, and distribution of goods that are determined by competition in a free market

class struggle: a struggle (sometimes violent) between the ruling class and the working class through which history moves from one stage to another. People identify and destroy the evils of the dominant class and then give power to the poorer classes.

Comintern: a word that is short for "Communist International," an international branch of Communism founded by Russian Vladimir Lenin in 1919

Communism: a governmental system that encourages the elimination of private property and the even distribution of goods to the public. A Communist government maintains central control over banking, business, housing, education, industry, medical care, the military, and regional security forces.

counterrevolutionary: a person who opposes revolution. Mao applied this term to anyone who disagreed with his policies.

Great Leap Forward: Mao Zedong's dramatic mass organization (1958–1961) to increase industrialization and productivity in China. The result of this drastic movement was economic disaster and widespread starvation.

Guomindang: the Chinese Nationalist Party founded by Sun Yat-sen in 1912

imperialism: the policy of extending the power of one nation to control another territory by invasion or by gaining indirect control of the political and economic systems

Manchu: a nomadic group of people from Manchuria who invaded China in 1644 and ruled until 1912

Marxism: the political, economic, and social principles of Karl Marx (1818–1883). Marxist theory promotes a classless society, the elimination of private ownership, and the provision of work, lodging, and food for all citizens.

Politburo: the central policy-making group of the Chinese Communist Party

propaganda: information spread to help one's cause or to hinder an opposing cause

republic: a country with leaders who are elected and are not monarchs

Socialism: a political theory promoting governmental ownership and administration of production and distribution of goods

PROMINENT CHINESE PEOPLE 1900–1976 AND PRONUNCIATION GUIDE

In order to write Chinese names in the Roman alphabet, scholars and diplomats use the pinyin system. The United Nations and other international organizations have adopted this system. The pinyin system is pronounced as it looks except that the letter *c* sounds like *ts*, and the letter *q* sounds like *ch*. In some cases, an apostrophe is used to distinguish a break in the pronunciation. The pinyin system is used in this book except in cases where names in an older romanization system are well known. Hyphens in many personal names have also been removed.

Chiang Kaishek	[jee-ahng ky-sheck] leader of the Nationalist Party
Deng Xiaoping	[duhng shee-ah-ow-pihng] former premier of China
He Zizhen	[huh zuh-jehn] third wife of Mao
Hua Guofeng	[hwah gwo-fuhng] former premier of China
Jiang Qing	[jee-ahng chihng] fourth wife of Mao Zedong
Lin Biao	[lihn bee-yow] military leader, early supporter of Mao
Liu Shaoqi	[lee-yoo shah-ow-chee] Communist Party organizer and leader
Mao Anlong	[mah-ow ahn-lohng] Mao's third son
Mao Anqing	[mah-ow ahn-chihng] Mao's second son
Mao Anying	[mah-ow ahn-yihng] Mao's first son
Mao Li Min	[mah-ow lee mihn] Mao's daughter
Mao Li Na	[mah-ow lee nah] Mao's youngest daughter
Mao Rensheng	[mah-ow rehn-sheng] Mao's father
Mao Zedong	[mah-ow dzuh-dohng] former chairman of People's Republic of China
Mao Zejian	[mah-ow dzuh-jee-yehn] Mao's adopted sister
Mao Zemin	[mah-ow dzuh-mihn] Mao's brother
Mao Zetan	[mah-ow dzuh-tahn] Mao's brother
Puyi	[poo yee] last Manchu emperor of China
Sun Yat-sen	[sun yaht-zehn] leader of China's republican revolution
Wen Qimei	[wehn chee-may] Mao's mother

Xiao Mao	[[shee-ah-ow mah-ow] Mao's fourth son
Xiao Yu (Siao-Yu)	[shee-ah-ow yew] Mao's close friend in youth
Yang Kaihui	[yahng ky-hway] Mao's second wife
Zhou Enlai	[joe ehn-lie] former premier of China
Zhu De	[jew du] commander in chief of the Red Army

SOURCES

7   Li Zhisui, *The Private Life of Chairman Mao*, trans. Tai Hung-chao (New York: Random House, 1994), 51.

8   Li, 52.

8   Mao Zedong, "Proclamation of the Central People's Government of the PRC, October 2, 1949" *Selected Works of Mao Tse-tung*, 2005, http://www.marxists.org/reference/archive/mao/selected-works/volume-7/mswv7_003.htm (July 6, 2005).

9   Philip Short, *Mao: A Life* (New York: Henry Holt, 1999), 419–420.

14 Edgar Snow, *Red Star over China* (1938; repr., New York: Grove Press, 1961), 126.

19 Mao Zedong, "Yellow Crane Tower," Spring 1927, *Selected Works of Mao Tse-tung*, http://www.marxists.org/reference/archive/mao/selected-works/poems/poems02.htm (July 6, 2005).

26 Short, 56.

26 Siao-yu (Xiao Yu), *Mao Tse-Tung and I Were Beggars* (Syracuse, NY: Syracuse University Press, 1959), 31.

26 Short, 70.

28 Siao-yu, 68.

30 Short, 93.

40 Lee Feigon, *Mao: A Reinterpretation* (Chicago: Ivan R. Dee, 2002), 47.

50 Mao Zedong. *Selected Works of Mao Tse-Tung*, vol. 1 (Peking: Foreign Languages Press, 1967), 147.

51 Mao Zedong, "On Practice: On the Relation between Knowledge and Practice, between Knowing and Doing," July 1937, *Selected Works of Mao Tse-tung*, 2004, http://www.marxists.org/reference/archive/mao/index.htm (July 6, 2005).

53 Short, 376.

59 Jonathon Spence, *Mao Zedong* (New York: Penguin Putnam, Inc., 1999), 107.

59 Short, 407.

59–60 Sidney Rittenberg and Amanda Bennett, *The Man Who Stayed Behind* (Durham, NC: Duke University Press, 2001), 111.

61 Mao Zedong, "The Chinese People Have Stood Up! September 21, 1949" *Selected Works of Mao Tse-tung*, 2004, http://www.marxists.org/reference/archive/mao/selected-works/volume-5/mswv5_01.htm (July 6, 2005).

62 Maggie Huang, e-mail interview with the author, April 15, 2003.

67 Geyshe Rinchen, letter to the author, October 25, 2003.

69 Short, 434.

69 Mao Zedong, "Report on an Investigation of the Peasant Movement in Hunan, March 1927," *Selected Works of Mao Tse-tung*, 2005, http://www.marxists.org/reference/archive/mao/selected-works/volume-1/mswv1_2.htm (July 6, 2005).

72 Sidney Rittenberg, interview with the author, October 3, 2003.

76 Li, 318.

81 "Talk by Chairman Mao Tse-tung," August 22, 1964, *The Spark* November 1991, http://home.clear.net.nz/pages/wpnz/maospeech.htm (July 6, 2005).

81 "Timeline of Nuclear Age, 1964," *NuclearFiles.org*, 2005, http://www.nuclearfiles.org/menu/timeline/1960/1964.htm (July 6, 2005).

84 Dr. Jin Wu, personal interview with the author, November 20, 2004.

85 Spence, 161.

94 Li, 612.

94 Short, 624.

BIBLIOGRAPHY

Chang, Jung, and Jon Halliday. *Mao: The Unknown Story*. London: Jonathan Cape, 2005.

Feigon, Lee. *Mao: A Reinterpretation*. Chicago: Ivan R. Dee, 2002.

Kau, Michael Y., and John K. Leung, eds. *The Writings of Mao Zedong, 1949–1976*. New York: M. E. Sharpe, Inc., 1986.

Lee, Lily Xiao Hong, and Sue Wiles. *Women of the Long March*. Saint Leonards, AU: Allen & Unwin, 1999.

Li Zhisui. *The Private Life of Chairman Mao*. Translated by Tai Hung-chao. New York: Random House, 1994.

Rittenberg, Sidney, and Amanda Bennett. *The Man Who Stayed Behind*. Durham, NC: Duke University Press, 2001.

——. *The Thought of Mao Tse-tung*. Cambridge, UK: Cambridge University Press, 1989.

Short, Philip. *Mao: A Life*. New York: Henry Holt, 1999.

Siao Yu (Xiao Yu). *Mao Tse-tung and I Were Beggars*. Syracuse, NY: Syracuse University Press, 1959.

Snow, Edgar. *Red Star over China*. 1938. Reprint, New York: Grove Press, 1961.

Spence, Jonathan. *Mao Zedong*. New York: Penguin Putnam Inc., 1999.

Zedong, Mao. *Chairman Mao Talks to the People. Talks and Letters: 1956–1971*. Edited by Stuart Schram. Translated by John Chinnery and Tieyun. New York: Pantheon Books, 1974.

——. *Selected Works of Mao Tse-Tung*. Peking: Foreign Languages Press, 1967.

FURTHER READING AND WEBSITES

BOOKS

Behnke, Alison. *China in Pictures*. Minneapolis: Lerner
Publications Company, 2003.

Da Chen. *China's Son: Growing Up in the Cultural Revolution*.
New York: Delacorte Press, 2001.

Fritz, Jean. *China Homecoming*. New York: G. P. Putnam's Sons,
1985.

Ji-li Jiang. *Red Scarf Girl: Memoir of the Cultural Revolution*. New
York: HarperCollins, 1997.

Lu Chi Fa. *Double Luck: Memoirs of a Chinese Orphan*. New
York: Holiday House, 2001

Siao-yu. *Mao Tse-tung and I Were Beggars*. Syracuse, NY:
Syracuse University Press, 1959

Stewart, Whitney. *Deng Xiaoping: Leader in a Changing China*.
Minneapolis: Lerner Publications Company, 2001.

———. *The 14th Dalai Lama*. Minneapolis: Lerner Publications
Company, 2000.

WEBSITES

East and Southeast Asia: An Annotated Directory of Internet
Resources, Mao Zedong
http://newton.uor.edu/Departments&Programs/
AsianStudiesDept/china-mao.html
This site contains an annotated list of Mao Zedong online
references.

Mao Zedong Reference Archive
http://www.marx.org/reference/archive/mao/index.htm
This Mao Zedong reference library includes essays, speeches, brief
biography, photographs, and links to sites with Mao's poetry.

Quotations from Chairman Mao Tse-tung
http://art-bin.com/art/omaotoc.html
This website provides quotations by Mao Zedong, which are
organized according to subject and most provide dates and
sources.

Stefan Landsberger's Chinese Propaganda Poster Pages
http://www.iisg.nl/~landsberger
This website displays Chinese propaganda posters and
illustrations from 1949 until the present day.
Travel China Guide
http://www.travelchinaguide.com/cityguides/hunan/
This site provides travel and geographical information for
Hunan Province and the city of Changsha, where Mao lived
before the establishment of the People's Republic of China.

INDEX

OTHER TITLES FROM LERNER AND A&E®:

Arnold Schwarzenegger
Ariel Sharon
Arthur Ashe
The Beatles
Benito Mussolini
Benjamin Franklin
Bill Gates
Bruce Lee
Carl Sagan
Chief Crazy Horse
Christopher Reeve
Colin Powell
Daring Pirate Women
Edgar Allan Poe
Eleanor Roosevelt
Fidel Castro
Frank Gehry
George Lucas
George W. Bush
Gloria Estefan
Hillary Rodham Clinton
Jack London
Jacques Cousteau
Jane Austen
Jesse Owens
Jesse Ventura
Jimi Hendrix
J. K. Rowling
John Glenn
Joseph Stalin
Latin Sensations
Legends of Dracula

Legends of Santa Claus
Louisa May Alcott
Madeleine Albright
Malcolm X
Mao Zedung
Mark Twain
Maya Angelou
Mohandas Gandhi
Mother Teresa
Napoleon Bonaparte
Nelson Mandela
Oprah Winfrey
Osama bin Laden
Pope John Paul II
Princess Diana
Queen Cleopatra
Queen Elizabeth I
Queen Latifah
Rosie O'Donnell
Saddam Hussein
Saint Joan of Arc
Thurgood Marshall
Tiger Woods
Tony Blair
Vladimir Putin
William Shakespeare
Wilma Rudolph
Winston Churchill
Women in Space
Women of the Wild West
Yasser Arafat

ABOUT THE AUTHOR

Whitney Stewart has traveled to Burma, China, India, Japan, Nepal, Tibet, and Europe to carry out research for her biographies. She has interviewed the 14th Dalai Lama of Tibet, Aung San Suu Kyi of Burma, and Sir Edmund Hillary, a New Zealand mountaineer. She lives with her husband and son in New Orleans, Louisiana. All of her books are listed on her website, www.whitneystewart.com.

WEBSITES

Website addresses in this book were valid at the time of printing. However, because of the nature of the Internet, some addresses may have changed or sites may have closed since publication. While the author and Publisher regret any inconvenience this may cause readers, no responsibility for any such changes can be accepted by the author or Publisher.